CW00922108

PENNINE WATERW

A Pictorial History of the
LEEDS & LIVERPOOL CANAL

by
Gordon Biddle

DALESMAN BOOKS
1977

£1.75

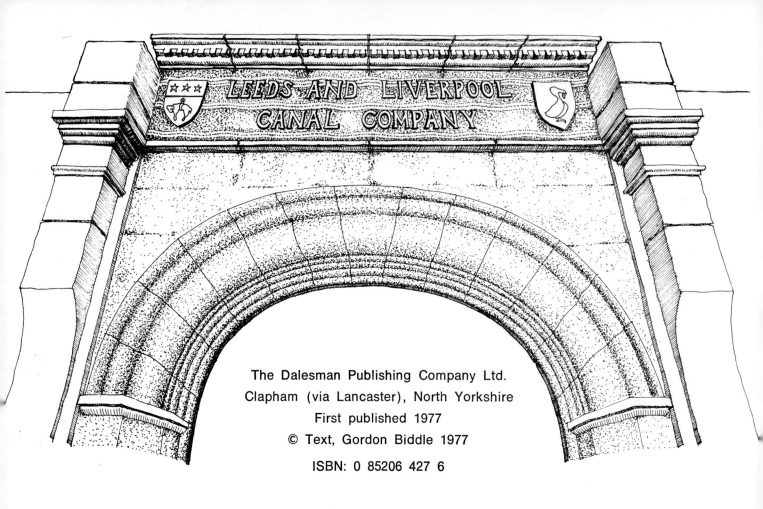

LEEDS AND LIVERPOOL
CANAL COMPANY

The Dalesman Publishing Company Ltd.
Clapham (via Lancaster), North Yorkshire
First published 1977
© Text, Gordon Biddle 1977
ISBN: 0 85206 427 6

Printed in Great Britain by Galava Printing Co. Ltd.
Hallam Road, Nelson, Lancs.

Contents

Drawings by Steve Burke. Map overleaf by Peter Fells, adapted from a map and section prepared by R. H. White, Engineer to the Company from 1897 to 1907.

The front cover is of the canal by the Anchor Inn, Salterforth, in 1907. The back cover shows Canal Transport Ltd. diesel barge **Wharfe** near Yarrow Bridge, Chorley, in 1940.

The drawing opposite is taken from a photograph by J. C. Parkinson of the Leeds & Liverpool Canal company's head office in Pall Mall, Liverpool, before demolition following war damage. The wavy lines represent water linking the arms of Leeds and Liverpool.

I

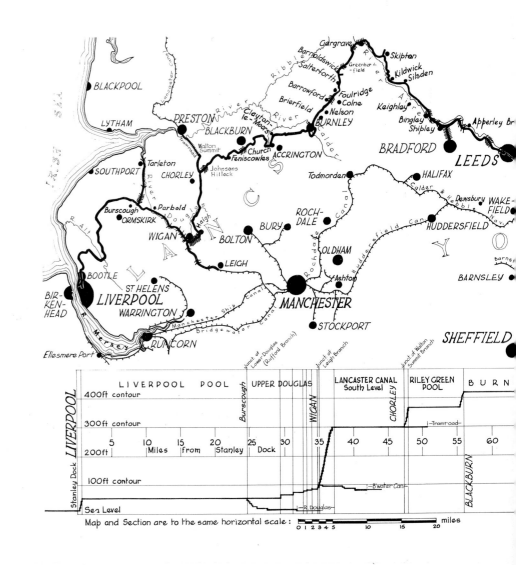

BLACKPOOL

LYTHAM

PRESTON

BLACKBURN

SOUTHPORT

Tarleton

CHORLEY

Burscough
ORMSKIRK

Parbold

WIGAN

BOLTON

LEIGH

BIR-
KEN-
HEAD

BOOTLE

ST. HELENS

LIVERPOOL

WARRINGTON

Ellesmere Port

RUNCORN

Gargrave

Barnoldswick

Salterforth

Greenber
-field

Skipton

Kildwick

Silsden

Barrowford

Brierfield

Foulridge

Colne

Nelson

Clayton-
le-Moors

Church

Feniscowles

ACCRINGTON

Keighley

Bingley

Shipley

Apperley Br

BURNLEY

Walton
Summit

Johnsons
Hillock

Haigh

BRADFORD

LEEDS

Todmorden

HALIFAX

ROCH-
DALE

BURY

OLDHAM

Ashton

Dewsbury

WAKE-
FIELD

HUDDERSFIELD

barnsl

BARNSLEY

MANCHESTER

STOCKPORT

SHEFFIELD

Junct of Lower Douglas
(Rufford Branch)

Junct of
Leigh Branch

Junct of
Leigh Branch

Junct of Walton
Summit Branch

LIVERPOOL POOL | UPPER DOUGLAS | LANCASTER CANAL
South Level | RILEY GREEN
POOL | BURN

400ft contour

300ft contour

Tramroad

5   10   15   20   25   30   35   40   45   50   55   60
Miles from Stanley Dock

200ft

100ft contour

B'water Can

R. Douglas

Sea Level

LIVERPOOL

Stanley Dock

Burscough

WIGAN

CHORLEY

BLACKBURN

Map and Section are to the same horizontal scale :

0 1 2 3 4 5   10   15   20   miles

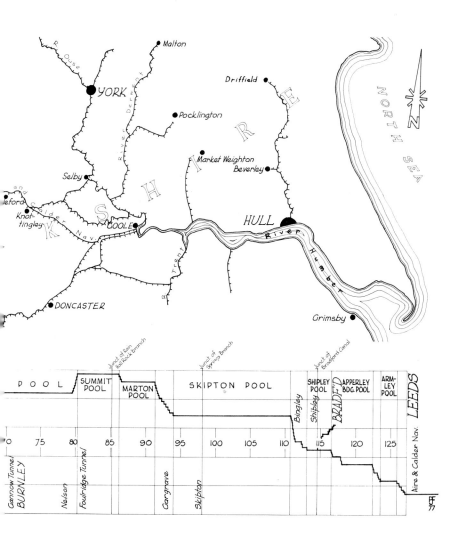

R. Ouse

• Malton

●YORK

River Derwent

• Driffield

R
I
V
E
R

R
I
D
I
N
G

NORTH SEA

• Pocklington

Y
O
R
K
S
H
I
R
E
S

Market Weighton
Beverley ●

Selby ●

Leeford
Knottingley ●

Canal & Calder Nav.

●GOOLE

HULL

River Humber

R. Trent

● DONCASTER

Grimsby ●

Junct. of Bain Hall Rock Branch

Junct. of Springs Branch

Junct. of Bradford Canal

| P O O L | SUMMIT POOL | MARTON POOL | SKIPTON POOL | | SHIPLEY POOL | | APPERLEY BDG. POOL | ARM-LEY POOL |

Bingley · Shipley · BRADFD · LEEDS

| 0 | 75 | 80 | 85 | 90 | 95 | 100 | 105 | 110 | 115 | 120 | 125 |

Gannow Tunnel
BURNLEY

Nelson

Foulridge Tunnel

Gargrave

Skipton

Aire & Calder Nav.

EF
77

The Leeds & Liverpool Canal

Three canals link Lancashire and Yorkshire across the Pennines: the Rochdale, the Huddersfield and the Leeds & Liverpool. Oldest of the trio and the longest single canal in Britain, only the Leeds & Liverpool is still navigable throughout, climbing 487 ft. through 92 locks in its 127 miles from the Mersey to the Aire which connects it with the Humber. Its variety in scenery is unequalled through the flat fen-like country of west Lancashire, the hills and moors of north-east Lancashire's cotton belt, the fringe of the Yorkshire Dales and the descent of the Aire valley to Leeds. With its broad sweeping curves, sturdy stone bridges, locks and warehouses, and above all its spectacular views, it not only epitomises traditional north-country waterways, but is by far England's finest canal.

Although two-thirds lie in Lancashire, the canal was conceived in Yorkshire. For many years its headquarters was in Bradford and its deviser and first engineer, John Longbottom, was a native of Halifax. Mid-eighteenth century Britain, commencing a hundred years of industrialisation, was still heavily dependent on the uncertainties of rivers and estuaries for much of its inland transport. Towns close to navigable water prospered; elsewhere the even greater uncertainties of atrocious roads and hill tracks made trade difficult and costly. In the north, packhorses provided the only trans-Pennine transport when Longbottom persuaded a Bradford wool merchant, John Hustler, that an east-west canal was feasible, using the low watershed between the Aire and the Ribble.

Canal promotion was starting to boom. The idea of a canal "uniting the east and the west seas" caught the imagination of businessmen and investors alike, and money was raised to float a company by Act of Parliament in 1770. Construction began that same year, simultaneously in Lancashire and Yorkshire. Four years later Liverpool was connected to Wigan by water and at the end of seven years' work Leeds was joined to Skipton, after which shortage of capital made further progress so sporadic that it was not until 1816, 46 years after the first ground had been broken, that a triumphant flotilla of decorated boats sailed from Leeds to Liverpool. Even then there was no connection with the Mersey until 1846. The canal was not only the country's longest; it also took the longest to build

Longbottom planned his original route to descend westward by following the lower reaches of the Lancashire Calder and the Ribble, passing south of Preston before striking out across west Lancashire to Ormskirk and Liverpool, but after internal disputes dissident Lancashire shareholders gained a longer but more lucrative route through the developing north-east Lancashire cotton towns. There were differences over dimensions, too. Locks are 14 ft wide throughout but from Liverpool to Wigan and on the Leigh branch are 72 ft. long to take Mersey barges and Midlands narrow boats, although on the remainder they are only 62 ft.

Leeds & Liverpool shareholders eventually owned one of the most prosperous canals in the country, receiving a dividend continuously from 1786 to 1919 which in the peak years 1843-1846 was as high as 34 per cent. Until the advent of the railways, the company exerted a powerful commercial influence in the north of England which, unlike so many other, poorer canal companies, was so firmly established and competitive that the newcomers took many years to dispel it. Then for 21 years from 1853 the canal allowed a consortium of railway companies to collect the revenue from merchandise traffic in return for a guaranteed fixed income, retaining only coal and mineral traffic in its own hands, with detrimental results. Although after 1874 the company managed to recover, things were never the same. In particular, through traffic dwindled, the average haul in 1906 being only 14 miles. Nonetheless, commercial carrying continued, albeit on a declining scale, right up to 1972 when the last regular cargoes — coal to Wigan — ceased.

Today the Leeds & Liverpool Canal is assuming a recreational rôle. With the establishment of boat clubs and hire-craft operators it is becoming increasingly popular as a holiday cruising waterway. The British Waterways Board does its best on maintenance despite a heavily subsidised, miniscule budget, so that from its waters the northern scene can be viewed from a completely different angle. The countryside along the canal is of high scenic quality, and to traverse parts of Burnley, Shipley or Leeds by water is like stepping back a century in time, a three-dimensional visual aid to appreciating what the Industrial Revolution was and did. Much is worthy of preservation in the towns; elsewhere at places like Church and Rishton enlightened urban renewal is long overdue. Blackburn, to its credit, has realised the canal's potential and plans to fully exploit its amenity value as part of a long-term development. Skipton, too, has already improved its waterside areas and now adds the canal to its many attractions. After all, local men built the canal, towns grew and prospered alongside it; surely it is only fitting that, its economic usefulness ended, visual and amenity qualities should take over. There is much to be proud of in the Leeds & Liverpool Canal.

Rollers were placed against bridge arches to prevent tow-lines chafing against the stonework.

Airedale

Leeds to Skipton

The canal leaves the River Aire at Victoria Bridge in the centre of Leeds and closely follows the river out through Kirkstall and Rodley to Shipley, Bingley, Keighley and Skipton, a distance of 29 miles with 29 locks. Many of them are in "staircases" where, instead of being separated by a stretch of water, two or more locks are placed together so that the top gate of one forms the bottom gate of the next. They are a particular feature of the Yorkshire side of the canal.

Beyond Kirkstall Abbey the route becomes surprisingly rural, the valley opening out to afford long, spectacular vistas as the canal steadily climbs its way above the river. Bingley is followed by a long lock-free length, or "pound", of 17 miles along the northern slopes, looking out across the valley to the high moors beyond. The Bingley - Skipton section was the first to be opened to navigation, on 8 April, 1773, when two boatloads of coal arrived in Skipton to sell at half the normal price. "The bells were set ringing . . .; there were also bonfires, illuminations and other demonstrations of joy." After three years' disruption of rural life as gangs af navvies dug the canal, quarries were opened for hewing stone and masons built walls, locks and bridges, the benefits of inland navigation were immediately apparent and the townsfolk had good cause to celebrate.

The canal office alongside Office Lock, Leeds.

River Lock, Leeds, junction with the Aire. The canal warehouse is on the left and to the right Aire & Calder coal barges are unloading at the Co-op wharf.

Just above River Lock a short branch passes under City station back into the river above the intervening weir to give access to wharves above. In the deep gloom of the Dark Arches, as they are aptly known, there is Arches (or Monk Pit) Lock and a short arm where the wooden-hulled dumb barge **Elvira** was photographed by flash in 1960, revealing the fine brick vaulting beneath the station.

Although there is a moored barge in this view of Rodley wharf it is being converted into living quarters and the warehouse which once stood alongside has gone. The white building is **The Rodley Barge** pub, reminder of a once-busy scene.

At Shipley the Bradford Canal once branched off to the left past the white-painted toll office and old boatmen's lodgings known as "The Barracks". The branch had a chequered history, opened in 1774, closed by court order in 1867 following gross pollution, re-opened in 1872 and finally closed in 1922. Nominally independent, it was promoted by Leeds & Liverpool men and was completely dependent upon it.

Stone from Bolton Woods quarries was a major traffic on the Bradford. Fletcher and Waterhouse's boat **Victoria**, with a cargo of cut stone, pauses to unhitch the horse at Old Venture Bridge in the 1890s.

The Bradford Canal had ten locks, all but one two-rise staircases. In the second phase of its existence water was pumped up to each pound from the one below, the locks distinguished by a steam pumping engine house and tall chimney like those in this picture of Spinkwell Locks about 1900.

Sootily dignified, this building in Manor Row, Bradford, was built as the head office of the Leeds & Liverpool Canal Company. After the removal to Liverpool in 1852 it was sold and in 1957 housed the York County Savings Bank. It has since had its stonework cleaned.

Right: The original Bradford terminus was at Broadstones, 3¼ miles from Shipley, shown in this painting by E. Crighton about 1865. The site is now beneath Forster Square, the canal having been cut back to Northbrook Street upon re-opening in 1872. Large wooden warehouses erected at that time still stand alongside Canal Road, itself a reminder of the past. Above: Today there are few traces of the Bradford Canal, although in 1955 most of the locks could still be seen derelict like Oliver Locks, with the old pumphouse on the left.

Top: The only sizeable aqueduct on the Leeds & Liverpool Canal is at Dowley Gap where the Aire is crossed between Saltaire and Bingley on eight low arches. Bottom, left: Before reaching the famous Five-rise Locks at Bingley there is a three-rise staircase which had this attractive lock cottage at the top. Unfortunately it has been demolished since this picture was taken in 1956. Bottom, right: An aqueduct at Kildwick which has an interesting dip in the middle to get the road under the channel.

Bingley Five-rise Locks, the largest of their type in England and one of the so-called wonders of the waterways, were opened in 1770 "to the amazement and delight" of several thousand spectators who watched the first boat descend in 29 minutes, to the accompaniment of cannon fired from the lock sides. They are shown here about 1906 with the old carpenters' shop and crane, now long gone, and on the right a new swivel bridge awaiting transport to its site. Presumably the horse on the skyline has just arrived with a boat.

Above: In 1925 Skipton wharf, at the junction with the Springs Branch, was a busy place. Here B. C. Walls' steamer **Beta** and diesel boat **Kappa** discharge. Left: Just beyond Skipton's Mill Bridge on the Springs Branch a flyboat discharges grain at Higher Mill in the late 1800s.

Above: More like a moat as it cuts around the back of Skipton Castle (right), the narrow Springs Branch terminates at loading chutes where until 1947 limestone from Haw Bank quarries was brought down a rope-worked railway incline. The branch was made by Lord Thanet in the 1770s and originally was served by a wooden tramway terminating at a staith on top of the tall stone buttresses seen in the background. As stone tipped from that height tended to go right through the bottom of a boat the incline and a lower staith were built in 1846. **Right:** Beyond the incline the railway ran alongside the Harrogate road in a stone cutting with a bridge under Embsay Road — now engulfed by road widening — before entering the quarries. From 1893 it was operated by steam locomotives.

Over the Summit

Skipton to Barrowford

From Skipton the canal follows the Aire a further four miles on the level before ascending the six Gargrave locks and turning south. It crosses the low hills by six more locks at Bank Newton and three at Greenberfield, where it attains its six-miles summit level and passes through the 1,640 yd.-long Foulridge Tunnel, opened in 1796, This section is one of the most beautiful as it winds between low, rounded hills in drumlin country, with long views east and west. From Gargrave to Barnoldswick it is also the loneliest, passing from Yorkshire into Lancashire.

Opposite, left: The unusual Double Bridge at East Marton is an example of the early engineers' caution. As the canal here traverses land sloping down from left to right, rather than risk a single lofty arch a lower one was incorporated to act as a buttress and take the thrust of the bank. When the steam launch **Dart** passed beneath in 1896, road traffic was a mere fraction of that now carried by the A59, yet the bridge still stands, although strengthened — a tribute to its builders.

Top, right: Higherland Lock, Gargrave, in the 1930s (sometimes called "Ireland" from local pronunciation), with the company's steam launch **Alexandra** probably taking directors on an inspection cruise.

Bottom, right: From the Bank Newton flight there are extensive views into the Craven dales. This picture shows the old carpenters' yard on the right, now a hire-craft centre. In company days it was customary to provide a free coffin for deceased employees, and the Bank Newton carpenters' daybook records that in January 1884 one was made for J. Harris, late clerk at Skipton.

1896

The early canals were built along the contours. Not only was it cheaper than making heavy embankments and cuttings but civil engineering was insufficiently advanced to risk them. There are some very sharp curves near East Marton, several requiring wooden rollers on posts to take the tow-line round without pulling the boat into the bank. One of the rollers had disappeared from this pair when the picture was taken, and now both posts, too, have gone.

In 1820 the single and two-rise locks at Greenberfield were replaced by three single locks on a short deviation. The old course can still be seen, including a bridge and the old lock cottage, in the centre of this picture which, from the type of bus, appears to date from the 1930s.

An unusual feature of the company's business activities was the extent to which it engaged in quarrying, initially to stimulate traffic on the new canal. In 1785 it leased the Skipton quarries and in 1796-99 made a short branch canal at Rain Hall near Barnoldswick. Although only half a mile long, it included two short tunnels, the second one seen here.

The branch was really a long quarry, water being let in behind the workings as cutting progressed so that stone could be loaded straight into the boats. In 1862 this remarkable viaduct was erected simply to connect the fields on each side — an indication of the value of the limestone trade to the company. Most of the branch remains, although the first few hundred yards have been obliterated, giving no indication from the main towing path of the hidden canal beyond.

It took five years to build Foulridge Tunnel, over half being on the "cut-and-cover" system due to the shallow depth and loose ground. Four times parts have collapsed, the last in 1902. Originally craft were "legged" through by professional leggers; they used the small building on the top. In 1880 a steam tug was provided, pictured here in 1918 emerging from the western portal while two boats wait to be taken back through.

Diesel boats reduced the need for the tug, which was withdrawn in 1937. Afterwards traffic was controlled by tunnel keepers using a telephone, and from 1957 to 1963 by these traffic lights operating on a time switch. The beam across the arch denotes the maximum headroom in the middle of the tunnel where the roof has dropped.

Left: Despite its seven reservoirs the Leeds & Liverpool was (and still is) chronically short of water in times of drought. One is at Rishton near Blackburn, five are close to the summit near Foulridge and Barrowford, and the sixth and largest, Winterburn, is in the fells north of Gargrave. A pipeline nearly nine miles long feeds the summit above Greenberfield top lock, marked by this brick recorder house. It was ceremonially opened by the chairman in 1893, using a silver key.

Right: At Barrowford, near Colne, the canal begins its descent from the summit by seven locks. Beside the top one stands this attractive cottage with the old toll office at the far end.

Cotton Country

Barrowford to Wigan

From Barrowford Locks to Burnley the canal is a demarcation line between town and country as it follows Pendle Water. The south-east bank is lined by the cotton mills of Nelson and Brierfield, while the opposite side has uninterrupted views across the valley to the commanding bulk of Pendle Hill (831 ft.). Beyond Burnley are more views on both sides, and between Clayton-le-Moors and Rishton the canal makes a great four-miles horseshoe to circumvent the Hyndburn valley and serve Church, which was the wharf for Accrington. In the area thereabouts cotton weaving, coal mining and quarrying once predominated, but now cotton retains only a foothold and the others have been replaced by newer industries. Yet mill towns like Blackburn and Burnley owe their development to the canal, which brought raw cotton from Liverpool docks and coal from local collieries, while the canal water itself was used for condensing steam from the countless engines which powered the mills.

After nearly 24 level miles the canal drops through six locks at Blackburn before passing into pleasantly rural surroundings again to a further group of seven at the picturesquely-named Johnson's Hillock. Here it joins what was originally the south end of the Lancaster Canal, which skirts Chorley and takes it on to the top of the great flight of 23 locks at Wigan.

Part of Slater Terrace, Burnley, an unusual row of early Victorian mill dwellings with an iron balcony overlooking the canal.

The famous Burnley embankment, nearly a mile long and 60 ft. high, carries the canal across the centre of the town. From below it looks like a railway embankment and at one time factories were built right up against it. A tunnel-like aqueduct took it over Yorkshire Street at the northern end, pictured here in the early 1920s before it was rebuilt. From the towing path there are panoramic views over the rooftops to the surrounding hills.

The embankment is perhaps best appreciated from Finsley Gate bridge at the south end. It is a clear demonstration of the rapid advance in civil engineering brought by canal building. In 1790 Robert Whitworth, the engineer at that time, constructed the meandering contour canal (page 20 top) to cross a shallow valley. Only five years later he boldly took it in a straight line across the valley at Burnley using in part the spoil from Gannow Tunnel a mile further on. Such were the fruits of experience.

Above: This late 19th century scene at Burnley's Manchester Road wharf shows typical Leeds & Liverpool warehouses. The oldest, on the right, was probably built about 1840, with progressive extensions as traffic increased, the later ones having protective canopies to enable susceptible cargoes like grain to be unloaded under cover.

Opposite: A good impression of the canal in its urban environment is given by this aerial view of Burnley showing it winding through a stone canyon of mills between Manchester Road (top) and Westgate.
To journey along this length is like stepping back 70 years in time.

Left: Until 1965 canal users had good reason to remember Moorfields colliery and coke ovens at Altham, near Accrington. Clouds of smoke and steam shot into the air as the retorts were charged. Now the site has been levelled for an industrial estate.

Right: Like Burnley, the canal's course through Blackburn is a graphic illustration of the 19th century Lancashire industrial scene. It is still largely an unchanged part of a town that is rapidly changing, although even this view up Blackburn Locks in 1966 is no longer the same following demolition of some of the mills.

Left: At the foot of the locks, Ewood embankment has this fine stone aqueduct, originally built to cross the River Darwen and a footpath. The path has grown into a road and the river has been squeezed into a culvert beneath it, forming a bridge under a bridge.

Right: In 1864 the Leeds & Liverpool leased the south end of the Lancaster Canal (see page 30 for earlier history). Because the latter was truncated from the main section north of Preston it had effectively been part of the Leeds & Liverpool for many years, of which the length from Johnson's Hillock to Walton Summit formed a branch, including the 259 yd. Whittle Hills Tunnel. After three collapses the centre section was opened out in 1838 to form two short tunnels, although the original width was retained between them. It was one of the earliest tunnels to have a towing path. Although the branch was disused after 1932 the tunnels were still passable when this photograph was taken in 1953.

Johnson's Hillock, near Chorley, is a reminder of the fierce rivalry between early canal companies. The Lancaster Canal, projected from Westhoughton to Kendal, was opened here in 1798, taking a course parallel to the one the Leeds & Liverpool later wished to use. Bitter wrangling went on until 1810 when the Leeds & Liverpool agreed to use the Lancaster between Johnson's Hillock and Wigan Locks, a case of "first come, first served". The Lancaster passes under the left-hand bridge on its way northward towards Preston; the Leeds & Liverpool enters the bottom lock on the right, towards Blackburn.

The Lancaster Canal Company never found the money to cross the Ribble valley by locks and an aqueduct, so between Walton Summit and Preston a horse tramway connected the two sections. Walton Summit had three basins, the central one covered by a two-span roof (the middle wall can be seen in this 1953 picture), and tramway tracks ran round the edges where transhipment took place. In 1968 the branch was filled in and Walton Summit itself obliterated by the M61 motorway.

A horse boat passes Whittle Springs brewery, near Chorley, in 1938.

Above: Lord Balcarres of Haigh Hall, near Wigan, was a prominent Lancaster Canal shareholder and provided much traffic from his Wigan Coal & Iron Co. The short branch shown here in about 1885, but now gone, led into his estate. The old Haigh Hall bridge is in the background.

Left: The Lancaster Canal tramway was sold to the Bolton & Preston Railway in 1837, which subsequently amalgamated with the North Union Railway. It kept the tramway open throughout until 1864, and from the Summit to Bamber Bridge until 1879. This cast-iron boundary post was still in position at the Summit in 1968.

Since 1960 the scene around Wigan Locks has changed radically. This view from the twelfth lock, half way up, shows the Whelley line railway bridge and, on the right, Rose Bridge colliery tips, both now disappeared.

Between the second and third locks at Wigan the Leigh Branch strikes off through the formerly busy colliery districts of Ince and Abram. It was opened in 1820. At Leigh are these typical Leeds & Liverpool warehouses. Beyond the bridge the canal makes an end-on junction with the Bridgewater Canal to form a through route to Manchester, Runcorn and the Midlands.

West Lancashire

Wigan to Liverpool

After leaving Wigan the canal takes a huge semi-circular sweep, first north-west down the narrow, wooded Douglas valley between Parbold Hill and Ashurst Beacon to Burscough, then south across the plain to Liverpool, making on its way a secondary detour up and down the shallow valley of the little River Alt, another sure sign that this was one of the first sections to be cut. There are five locks down from Wigan; Pagefield was inserted in 1904 to counteract subsidence, after which Crooke was removed for the same reason. Ell Meadow, Dean and Appley were duplicated to speed up traffic, the last by a pair of locks alongside a single 12 ft. deep lock. Now only one is in use at each of the three places. A short stub on the north side at Parbold is a reminder that there the intended course via the Ribble valley would have joined the present route, the only physical evidence of Longbottom's original scheme.

Market gardening and smallholdings typify the flat landscape of the 15 miles from Parbold to Maghull where suburban Merseyside is encountered, although not until Litherland does the scene become industrial. Here, too, a familiar feature of north Liverpol's skyline joins the canal — a long series of electricity pylons which straddle it from Clarence Dock power station. Although close to Bootle and Liverpool docks, the canal is out of sight until a short branch drops down four locks into Stanley Dock and then out through Colling-

wood and Salisbury Docks into the Mersey. The main canal continues for a further half mile between tall warehouses and Tate & Lyle's sugar refinery to terminate abruptly at Chisenhale Street bridge, the last quarter mile to the old terminus in Pall Mall and the appropriately-named Leeds Street having been filled in during the late 1950s.

Stone-built toll office at No. 4 lock, Johnson's Hillock.

The last horse-drawn trip —
H. & R. Ainscough's boat
Parbold is hauled out of Appley
Lock on a misty day in 1960.

Although there is now nothing
to suggest that the shallow,
winding River Douglas once
took boats up to Wigan, it was
in fact a forerunner of the canal.
It was made navigable from the
Ribble estuary between 1733
and 1742, with a number of
short-cuts and locks. The
remains of some are still
traceable; this is one at Dean.

In 1771 the Leeds & Liverpool bought the Douglas Navigation and replaced it by a parallel canal from Burscough to Wigan which eventually became part of the main line. Then in 1781 the lower Douglas was superseded by what is now known as the Rufford Branch, leaving the main canal near Burscough and falling by eight locks to join the tidal Douglas at Tarleton. In 1965 the branch was in such poor condition that this notice on the top lock at Lathom warned that maximum depth was only two feet. Now it is much improved.

Until 1805 the Rufford Branch joined the Douglas at Sollom Lock. Then a new river channel was made and the canal extended through the old one to a new tide lock at Tarleton. Sollom's gates were removed but the old lock chamber remains.

Between Tarleton, the Ribble estuary and the sea lie some four miles of tidal river. When the West Lancashire Railway was built in 1882 a swing bridge was necessary to allow sailing barges to pass beneath on the tide. For five years a **River Douglas station** appeared in the timetable. It had no road access and seems to have been intended for a paddle steamer service which apparently operated on the river for a time. The railway was closed in 1964 and the bridge dismantled.

Beneath the broad skies of the West Lancashire plain the diesel boats **Progress** and **Margaret** pass Scarisbrick, bound for Liverpool.

A feature marking the canal's entry into Liverpool was the electrically operated lift bridge at Litherland, built in 1922 to replace a wooden bridge, and itself replaced by a high-level bridge in 1975. When the canal was busy it was a notorious bottleneck for road traffic.

Liverpool Locks fall 44 ft. to Stanley Dock, passing beneath the rail approaches to Exchange station.

In 1960 Ainscoughs' motor boat **Burscough 2** passes through Stanley Dock breasted up to the dumb barge **Claymore**, heading for the canal locks under the arch in the distance.

Right: At Chisenhale Street bridge the canal virtually passes through Tate & Lyle's refinery in a dark chasm. Here coal boats await unloading in 1958. On the opposite side suction pipes project over the water for unloading dry cargoes.

Above: Beyond, the last short stretch of canal is now only a memory. In this picture taken in 1960, filling-in has started.

Opposite: Liverpool Corporation refuse destructor received coal by canal, with its own arm in Charters Street, seen here in 1906.

Traffic

In the canal age everything possible went by water. The promoters of the Leeds & Liverpool saw their canal as a means of opening up the country between the two cities to develop industry and trade, "some parts abounding with best coal, but destitute of lime-stone; while, in other parts . . . inexhaustible rocks of the best lime-stone, but a total want of coal". Elsewhere there was ". . . slate, flags, timber fit for ship-building and for common buildings. The whole intermediate country between Leeds and Liverpool . . . will be supplied with wool, woollen yarn, corn and provisions, hides, tallow, linen, tin-plates, deal, timber, board, planks, iron, hemp, flax, potash, and whatever else is imported . . . These are part of the very great and almost inconceivable benefits which will arise to the whole intermediate country." Thus wrote John Hustler in 1768.

At first, canal companies were precluded from operating their own boats, being regarded as providers of a waterway on which others could trade in return for payment of a toll per ton-mile, varying according to commodity. Later they were allowed to carry in their own right alongside private traders.

The Leeds & Liverpool developed a very efficient and extensive goods-carrying organisation with agents in all the principal towns in Lancashire and Yorkshire, and beyond. Large new warehouses were built and "fly boats" introduced, operating to a timetable with priority over other craft on the canal. Fleets were also operated by firms of carriers, colliery companies and other industries with waterside premises, while there were always "number ones", the owner-boatmen who plied for hire and would carry anything.

Top, left: Coal for power stations was a mainstay in the canal's later years of commercial operation. A special "loop" and wharf were made for Kirkstall power station, Leeds, in 1928, but were disused by the 1960s.

Top, right: The wooden boat **Helen** loads at Bickershaw Colliery on the Leigh Branch in 1956.

Bottom: Blackburn's Whitebirk power station had a special unloading wharf for coal from Bank Hall Colliery, Burnley, which succumbed to rail and road competition in the big freeze of 1963. This view of boats unloading was taken in 1958.

Atholl Street gas works, Liverpool, received coal by canal until 1964. It is shown here in 1958, with the electricity pylons well in evidence.

The final regular traffic was coal to Westwood power station, Wigan, which ceased in 1972. Since then there has been no regular commercial carrying on the canal.

Only large industrial premises had special unloading facilities.
Elsewhere coal had to be shovelled and barrowed, as at Audley Mill,
Blackburn, in the 1930s.

This page: Top: Domestic coal, too, went by canal, many merchants having their own boats, like John Robert Thornton of Skipton, seen here aboard his steamer with Bill Hesketh. Bottom: Grain was another important cargo. H. & R. Ainscough Ltd. of Burscough had an extensive fleet operating to Liverpool, Birkenhead and Manchester. Their mill, pictured here in 1958, was well equipped for canal traffic.

Opposite: Top, right: Corn millers and soap manufacturers had canal-side premises at Clayton-le-Moors. By the time this picture was taken in the late 1960s Appleby's mill had closed and has since been demolished. Left: In 1877 Benjamin Curry Walls was born in Higherland Lock-house, Gargrave, son of a Leeds & Liverpool traffic regulator. In 1919 he set up as a canal carrier with one boat and a horse. By 1930 the B. C. Walls fleet comprised 18 diesel boats, when the firm amalgamated with three others to form Canal Transport Ltd., in which the Leeds & Liverpool had a majority shareholding. Bottom, right: Some of the Walls fleet frozen up at Skipton.

A laden company fly-boat enters Greenberfield top lock.

A pair of fly-boats unload cotton at Church wharf, near Accrington, about 1930.

A steam fly-boat acts as tug for a string of laden boats passing a diesel boat near Chorley in 1935.

Typical of the company's large warehouses are those built for wool at Shipley, photographed in 1974 after cleaning.

Blackburn had a large depot at Eanam, the newer part of which was built for grain traffic. The office building has an interesting curved end.

For 36 years the canal from Liverpool terminated at Wigan, where this large stone warehouse was built. A British Waterways "River" class boat is shown leaving in 1957.

Bank Hall warehouse, Liverpool, was erected in 1874, copying railway practice. An arm of the canal went inside, and a large wooden shed and a covered wharf adjoined.

Top, left: In country districts small warehouses were built, of which this stone building at Barrowford is typical, with an office and lock-keeper's cottage, now sadly derelict, alongside.

Top, right: The last cargo from Bradford leaves in B. C. Walls' steamer **Beta** in 1921. Canal Road wharves and warehouses are in the background.

Bottom: Close proximity to Aintree racecourse gave opportunities not to be missed. On Grand National days a box for company officials was mounted on a mud hopper near Canal Turn.

It is not commonly realised that before railways the canals carried considerable passenger traffic. Regular packet boat services connected all main centres with light, fast vessels drawn by two or more horses at a canter, with a postillion. They had top priority and usually had first and second class cabins, heating and refreshments — a big advance on the cold, bumpy stage-coaches. Here the Liverpool - Wigan packet drops its tow-line to pass under the old Chisenhale Street bridge.

LEEDS AND LIVERPOOL CANAL CO.

NOTICE
FOULRIDGE TUNNEL
Alteration of working hours of Tug

On and after WEDNESDAY, APRIL 23rd, 1930, the Tug will leave when required:—

From the FOULRIDGE end of Tunnel:

MONDAY
TUESDAY | At the hours of 7 a.m., 9 a.m.,
WEDNESDAY | 11 a.m., 1 p.m., 3 p.m., and
THURSDAY | 5 p.m.
FRIDAY |

SATURDAY - 7 a.m., 9 a.m. and 11 a.m.

SUNDAY - - 10 a.m., if necessary

From the BARROWFORD end of the Tunnel:

MONDAY
TUESDAY | At 8 a.m., 10 a.m., 12 noon, 2 p.m.,
WEDNESDAY |
THURSDAY | 4 p.m. and 6 p.m.
FRIDAY |

SATURDAY - 8 a.m., 10 a.m. and 12 noon

SUNDAY - - 11 a.m., if necessary

CANAL OFFICE, LIVERPOOL
April 22nd, 1930.

ROBT. DAVIDSON,
General Manager and Engineer.

BY ORDER

CAUTION.
ENTERING FOULRIDGE TUNNEL WITHOUT A PERMIT.

NOTICE IS HEREBY GIVEN that at the Colne Police Court on Wednesday, 21st September 1921, the captain of a Motor Boat was **CONVICTED OF ENTERING OR PASSING THROUGH THE TUNNEL AT FOULRIDGE WITHOUT A PERMIT FIRST OBTAINED FROM AN AUTHORISED AGENT OF THE COMPANY AND WAS ORDERED TO PAY £2. 17s. FOR FINE AND COSTS.**

All similar offenders will be prosecuted.

BY ORDER, **FRANK H. HILL,**

Bradford, September 1921. Law Clerk to the Company.

Opposite: Top, left: For working horse boats through Foulridge and Gannow tunnels two steam tugs were built. To avoid the need to turn at each end the vessels were fitted with dual propellers, tillers and controls so that they could be steered from both ends. In later years the Foulridge tug had compressed air cylinders to combat smoke and fumes in the tunnel. It is seen here at the east end in 1941, in use for inspection purposes after withdrawal from regular service in 1937. Top, right: With the introduction of diesel boats there was less need for tugs and in 1930 notice was given of a reduction in service at Foulridge. Bottom: As there was no space for boats to pass in the tunnel, strict regulation of entry was necessary. Infringement of the bye-laws incurred penalties which were publicised as a warning to others.

This page: Top: Canal cruises are not new. The canal was popular for Sunday School outings and such like, as shown by this picture of two heavily-laden fly-boats and a horse-boat, complete with photographer, ready to leave Clayton-le-Moors about 1900. Bottom: The rail excursion and the motor coach had not won a complete monopoly even by 1926 when Walls' steamer **Lambda**, complete with tarpaulin awning, prepared to leave Skipton with B. C. Walls on the bow.

Boats and Boatmen

Craft able to work through the 62 ft. locks from Wigan to Leeds were known as "shortboats", traditionally built with well-rounded bows and a square transom stern, although company boats had rounded sterns. The wooden horse-boats had a cabin fore and aft, capable of housing one or two families. Compared with the narrow Midlands canals pay was good, there was little overcrowding and boat families were regarded as hard-working, respectable people. Each cabin had a stove (Yorkshire-built craft distinguished by a square chimney), a folding table-cum-cupboard door, benches and recessed bunks. The boats carried up to 50 tons.

The introduction of steamers in 1880 meant dispensing with the stern cabin to make space for an engine and boiler compartment, but the reduction in cargo space was more than compensated by the steamers' ability to tow one or more dumb barges or "butties", which themselves provided more cabin space. They also enabled an improved fly-boat service to be operated between Liverpool and Leeds in three days, including night travel. In later years many crews lived on the land, working a roster system and changing over at an appointed place from which they worked another boat back home. The canal company eventually owned 30 steamers powered by four-cylinder compound engines in "V" form without condensers — true "puffers" exhausting their steam straight up their chimneys. They had coal-fired Field vertical water-tube boilers, and were so successful that within ten years the company had dispensed with all its horses.

In the late 1920s diesel engines were tried, first in converted steamers and then in purpose-built craft, so that by the mid-1930s the remaining steamers were all in independent hands where they lasted until the 1950s. The most popular diesel engines were single or twin-cylinder Widdops and Gardners. Steel boats also appeared in the 1930s. Canal Transport Ltd. built a "River" class boat, followed in 1950 by British Waterways' "Town" class, but wooden boats continued to be built for independent operators until about 1955.

Leeds & Liverpool boats were not so highly decorated as the traditional Midlands narrow boats, but even so were attractively painted with scroll and floral designs in bright colours. Independent fleet owners had their own liveries; Ainscoughs', for instance, had red hulls.

With the demise of family boats a crew was usually a captain, mate and boy, the men leading the horse or steering and the boy going on ahead to prepare locks. The introduction of diesels eventually led to many boats being single-manned.

Above: A square-sterned Yorkshire shortboat in Riders' dock, Leeds, in the 1950s; **Wire No. 3**, owned by Leeds Corporation Electricity Department. Right: Another wooden shortboat on the company's stocks at Finsley Gate yard, Burnley.

Top, left: Away from her home
waters the **Anthony** of Airedale
Canal Services Ltd. is towed
past Scarisbrick by "River"
class diesel **Nidd** in 1959.
Bottom, left: Company steamers
Beaver, Amy and **Agate** with
their crews at Bingley.
Top, right: Vessels changed
hands sometimes by public
auction, like this one advertised
in 1834.

Above: The Leeds & Liverpool had a number of tugs in addition to its cargo-carrying steamers. Here No. 57 waits at the top of Bingley Five-rise Locks. Right: The diesel boat **Progress** is one-man operated near Scarisbrick in 1958.

There were boat-builders' yards at numerous places, generally characterised by a long open-sided shed from which boats could be launched sideways, like **Peter** here being re-launched from J. & T. Hodson's yard at Whitebirk, Blackburn, after repairs.

A new steel hopper barge is launched with a splash at the canal company's Apperley Bridge depot.

Inside Mayors' boat-building shed at **Tarleton**, on the **Rufford Branch**, in 1957, a barge is being re-planked. A mixture of tallow and soft soap was used to grease the slip for launching. Mayors originally built sailing barges, or "flats", for trading up the coast to West Cumberland.

Most of the builders have now gone, but Mayors' yard is still busy with canal and sea-going pleasure craft. Since this picture in 1958 the scene has become even more animated, with craft lining both banks.

The company owned several steam launches for official purposes, one of the best known being **Waterwitch.** Many a management committee meeting was held aboard her, probably such an occasion when this picture was taken at Bingley, complete with white-aproned steward.

Waterwitch was a graceful craft, built in the tradition of the river steamers and seen here again at Bingley. She was present at the official opening of Winterburn Reservoir in 1893, was still used for meetings in 1945 when one was held at Leigh, and survived into British Waterways' ownership.

Alexandra, seen here at Newlay in 1906, was smaller and probably used for official inspections.

Victoria was bought second-hand in 1898 for £125, for the use of Lancashire officers, and was chiefly used as an engineer's survey boat. She had a beautifully-shaped and carved prow but must have been inconvenient in wet weather. A smaller steam launch, **Dart**, was purchased for the Yorkshire side.

Dick Draper was captain of Foulridge Tunnel tug from 1897 until its withdrawal in 1937, when he was photographed for the occasion.

Top, left: The crew of **Waterwitch** and a company official (centre) pose for a photograph. Top, right: Among the last boat couples were Mr. and Mrs. Tommy Carrington. His nickname "Tommy Ninetoes" needs no explanation. Bottom: Women worked as crews in the 1939-45 war. Here recruits are instructed in rope work in 1942, under the eye of B. C. Walls.

Maintaining the Canal

The Engineering Department of a major canal company was one of the most important, responsible for the maintenance of structures, locks and bridges; regulating the water supply; dredging the channel and repairing the banks and towing path; and numerous other jobs essential in ensuring the movement of traffic. Maintenance yards were established at a number of places on the Leeds & Liverpool, comprising carpenters' shop, smithy, engineering shop, stables and stores. The carpenters in particular were vital to the canal and could produce anything from fencing posts to lock gates or a barge. In the early 1920s 13 carpenters were employed at Apperley Bridge depot alone.

For maintenance purposes the canal was divided into sections, each controlled by a divisional superintendent or engineer. In 1865, for instance, there were four between Leeds, Barnoldswick, Chorley, Dean Lock and Liverpool respectively. In 1894 the department had 131 craft of various kinds, including seven steam dredgers. Hours were long and pay low. In 1899 the bankrangers asked for a rise. Foremen were receiving 4s (20p) and their men 3s. 4d (16½p) for an 11½ hour day, often involving a long walk to and from their workplace for which there was no payment. But at least the work was regular and in many cases sons succeeded fathers through several generations.

Opposite: Locks are filled and emptied by sluices controlled by wooden "paddles" or, as they are called on northern canals, "cloughs" (pronounced "clows"). To speed the flow of water in and out there are gate paddles opening and closing a square aperture near the foot of the gate, and ground paddles controlling a culvert running behind the lock walls. The Leeds & Liverpool has an exceptionally interesting variety of paddle gear.

Shown here are: Top, left: A pair of primitive yet effective ground paddles called "jack cloughs" at Greenberfield, opened by lifting the handle.
Centre: A screw-type ground paddle worked by a windlass, with a simple brake to control it when being dropped, also at Greenberfield.
Top, right: A fairly standard gate paddle worked by rack and pinion.
Bottom: A geared rack and pinion paddle needing a separate windlass or "key". The last is at Blackburn where the adjacent bridge allows insufficient clearance for the normal balance beam, and an unusual quadrant gear has been installed to operate the gate.

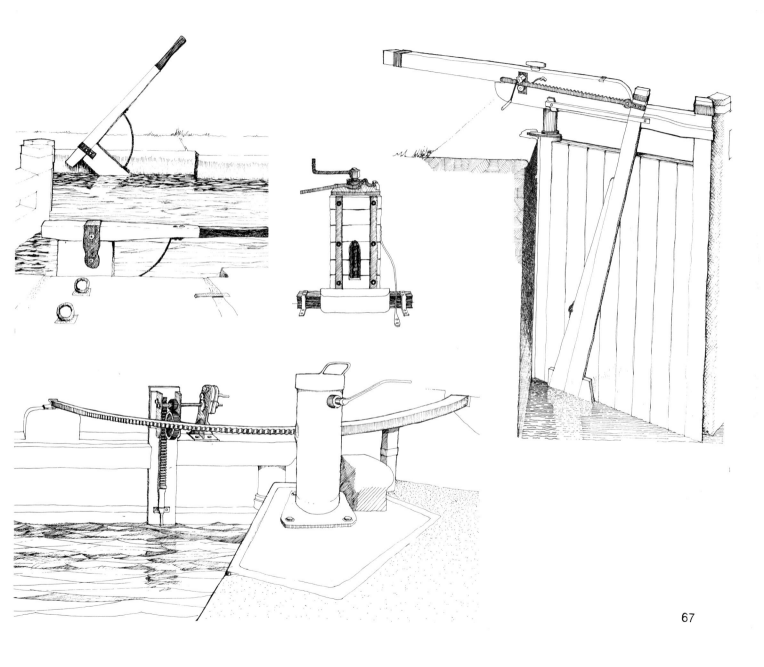

Opposite: Top, left: The canal at Bingley, drained for the replacement of the bottom gate sills, leaving three maintenance boats high and dry — then, as now, attracting a juvenile audience. Top, right: Sheer legs were used for replacing lock gates. In this view of Bingley Five-rise about 1900 the old bottom gate has been lifted out to rest on a barge while the bowler-hatted foreman takes his lunch precariously seated over the middle of the lock.
Bottom: At Easter 1906 the canal was drained at Newlay for lock repairs. The wooden trough on the left carries away water from the bye-wash running down from the upper pound.
The steamer is **Ada**.

This page: Top: Swivel bridges were produced in the company's workshops. Here the inspection launch **Dart** is being used as a tug to haul a new bridge to its site aboard a dumb barge.
Bottom: The carpenters had their own boats for site work, some named after places on the canal. This one is **Five Rise**, on a job at Kildwick in 1890.

Opposite: Top, left: The workshops were well equipped with power machinery like this horizontal saw at Finsley Gate yard, Burnley, in 1907. Top, right: Tools changed very little over the years. Here a balance beam is being prepared in Apperley Bridge workshops in 1936. Bottom: Special "houseboats" were provided for men working away from home. Houseboat No. 2 is seen here moored at Salterforth, with residents.

This page: Top: Where there was no natural means of draining a pound, a pump boat was used. Stop gates were provided at intervals — later replaced by removable planks in slots. The pump suction was dropped over one side of the gate, the steam regulator opened and water discharged on the other. This operation was usually a weekend job, and attracted a crowd of spectators.
Bottom: Dredging by hand-operated scoop was slow and laborious, and had to be done between passage of boats. The busy Enfield wharf, at Clayton-le-Moors, is the scene of this job about 1900.

Steam dredger No. 11 moored near Riley Green in 1910.

This steam dredger is discharging into a dumb barge which is then taken across the cut and emptied on to a tip by a steam grab.

Ice-breaking was spectacular for onlookers but back-breaking for the men. A special ice-breaker, narrow and iron-sheathed, was drawn at a brisk trot by anything up to 12 horses. On board two gangs of men faced each other, grasping a central rail or rope and rocking the boat from side to side to break up the ice. Only two horses were needed for thin ice at East Marton on this occasion.

In this picture near Farnhill, probably in the 1920s, the ice-breaker appears to have heeled over and stuck fast.

Steam tugs sometimes were used to follow the ice-breaker when conditions were particularly bad. No. 57 is seen here with an ice boat in 1924.

When out of use the ice-breakers were submerged to preserve their timbers, although this one at Niffany, near Skipton, in 1958 has probably been raised and sunk for the last time.

Many town bridges needed widening as traffic increased. Burlington Street bridge, Liverpool, was reconstructed in 1904.

While Shuttleworth House bridge, Hapton, was being rebuilt in the early 1900s a temporary wooden bridge was erected.

In 1926-27 Yorkshire Street aqueduct, Burnley, was rebuilt. Its narrow, low arch (right, top) was a notorious bottleneck, and during replacement, road traffic, including trams, had to continue uninterrupted, so a temporary wooden trough was built to take the boats across. The view opposite shows the trough under construction alongside the old aqueduct. When the work was completed (right, bottom) and shuttering removed, the new reinforced concrete aqueduct was revealed, complete with Union Jack motifs in the parapet. The actual water channel is carried in an iron trough.

Left: Sometimes disaster strikes, such as the violent storm in the Skipton area on 3 June, 1908, when Eller Beck flooded and burst into the Springs Branch, sweeping down to the main canal and flooding the lower part of the town. After boats had been brought up to load the debris the branch was drained for repairs.
Above: A new concrete retaining wall was built to keep out the beck, nearing completion in this picture, which also shows two of the tramway wagons above the loading chutes.

Opposite: Wartime air raids on Merseyside breached the canal several times and destroyed the company's head office. A direct hit at Sandhills in 1940 included four boats in its toll but fortunately missed the overhead power lines.

Acknowledgements

I am indebted to many individuals and organisations for the loan of photographs, as listed below, but I must particularly thank Mrs. Agnes Walls of Bingley and Miss Jane Harding of the Craven Museum, Skipton, for permission to use pictures from the late Norman Walls' collection, and to Jack Parkinson of Southport for his now unique photographs taken while the canal was still commercially active in the late 1950s. I must especially thank John Freeman of British Waterways, Edward Paget-Tomlinson and Harry Mayor for their help, Steve Burke for the drawings, John and Ronnie Pye of Clitheroe for photographic work, Peter Fells for the map and Charles Hadfield for the loan of the original on which it was based. The photographs have been supplied by the following individuals and collections. Figures relate to page numbers; B=bottom, L=left, R=right, T=top:

T. N. Walls collection and Craven Museum: Front cover, 15, 16, 19, 20B, 22T, 46T, 47TL, 47B, 48T, 52TR, 52B, 54, 55B, 57B, 58TR, 58B, 59L, 60, 62B, 63, 64, 65, 68, 69, 70, 72B, 73T, 74T, 78R.

G. Biddle and collection: 9T, 10, 12B, 13L, 14, 17, 20T, 21, 23, 25B, 28R, 29, 30, 32L, 35B, 36, 43TL, 48B, 50, 51B, 52TL, 72T.

J. C. Parkinson: 9B, 22B, 33, 35T, 37, 39, 41, 43TR, 43B, 44, 46B, 51T, 58TL, 59R, 62T, 74B.

Bradford Museums: 12T, 13R.

Leeds City Libraries: 57T.

G. Ingle: 11.

J. K. Ellwood: 73B.

J. E. Weatherill: 78L.

Burnley Public Library: 25T, 26, 27.

E. W. Paget-Tomlinson: 61.

J. Freeman: 75B, 76, 77, 79.

Clayton-le-Moors Civic Society: 28L, 47TR, 55T.

Bolton Evening News: Back cover, 31, 49.

Skipton Public Library: 71T.

Accrington Public Library: 32R, 71B.

Merseyside County Museums: 38.

Liverpool City Engineer's Department: 40, 75T.

Liverpool City Library: 53.

Blackburn District Libraries: 45.